THINK ON
THESE THINGS

Selections from the
Edgar Cayce Readings

A.R.E.® Press • Virginia Beach • Virginia

ISBN 87604-132-2

13th Printing, September 1989

Printed in the U.S.A.

CONTENTS

"*Think* on these things. For here ye may find not only the key to thine nature but that which may unlock the. . .mysteries of life itself in relationship to thy dealing with thy fellow man."

(Reading number 954-1)

FOREWORD

People often went to Edgar Cayce for relief from physical problems. His readings not only prescribed treatments to relieve their ills but also gave them inspiring words to uplift and comfort their minds and spirits.

The mental and spiritual guidance was universal, speaking to the higher self in each person. *Think on These Things* is a collection of some of these readings that can help you find comfort, guidance and inspiration every day. . .

"Be *glad* you have the opportunity to be alive at this time, and to be a part of that preparation for the coming influences of a spiritual nature that *must* rule the world. These are indicated, and these are part of thy experience. Be happy of it, and give thanks daily for it."

(Reading number 2376-3)

Of the Mind
and the Soul

For the mind is both spiritual and physical in its attributes to the human body, and if ye feed thy body-mind upon worldly things, ye become worldly. If ye feed thy mind upon those things that are His, ye become His indeed.   1299-1

For the very fact that ye find yourself conscious of being alive, of being capable of suffering disappointments, capable of being aware of missing something within thine own experience in the present—disappointed in people, disillusioned with your own family—should make you aware that God is mindful of thee and that thou hast forgotten God. Then in thy spiritual life, in thy spiritual purpose lies the answer in thy problems, physical, mental, material, spiritual. For when ye have set thine own house in order, regardless of what others may say, begin to read first the 19th of Exodus and the 5th verse, and see in whom ye may trust, where thy mind and thy soul may find rest. Consider what spirit, what purpose, what desire must occupy thy mind.

3506-1

The more and more each is impelled by that which is intuitive, or the relying upon the soul force within, the greater, the farther, the deeper, the broader, the more constructive may be the result.

792-2

. . .for he that seeks the Lord must believe that He is, would they find Him; for one doubting has already builded that barrier that prevents the proper understanding, whether as to physical, mental or spiritual attributes, or spiritual aid, or mental aid, or physical aid; for that in faith sought for shall be thine, even as was given, "Be my people and I will be your God."

459-1

In the first cause, or principle, all is perfect. In the creation of soul, we find the portion may become a living soul and equal with the Creator. To reach that position, when separated, must pass through all stages of development, that it may be one with the Creator.

900-10

. . .in the consciousness of eternity, time is not, neither is space. In man's consciousness there appears so much mercy, so much love that these have been called time and space.   3660-1

In the manner, the way ye attend, ye treat or ye hold—in thy mental self—thy brother's position, or thy neighbor's or thy friend's as thy own, *that* is the manner, the concept ye hold of thy Creator!

1603-1

Arguments gain little. The mental attitude and prayers gain much; for thoughts are things and their vibrations reach those in every sphere and walk of life as related to self and to others.   1438-2

Ideas may be as thoughts, made criminal or miracles. Be sure the *ideal* is proper. Follow that irrespective of outside influence. Know self is right, and then go straight ahead.   1739-6

Each entity is a part of the universal whole. All knowledge, all understanding that has been a part of the entity's consciousness, then, is a part of the entity's experience. Thus the unfoldment in the present is merely becoming *aware* of that experience through which the entity, either in body or in mind, has passed in a consciousness.   2823-1

Know thy ideal, and live to that. For, each soul must give account for its own self.   2803-2

For, what is the source of all healing for human ills? From whence doth the body receive life, light, or immortality? ...the body as an active force is the result of spirit and mind. . .Each soul has within its power that to use which may make it at one with Creative Forces or God. These are the sources from which life, light, and the activity of body, mind and soul may manifest in whatever may be the active source or principle in the mind of the individual entity. . .

There are, then, as given, those influences in the nature of man that may supply that needed. For, man in his nature—physical, mental and spiritual—is a replica, is a part of whole universal reaction in materiality.

Hence there are those elements which if applied in a material way, if there is the activity with same of the spirit and mind, may bring into the experience of each atom of the body force or cell itself the awareness of the Creative Force or God. It may only rise as high as the ideal held by the body-mind.

Hence there is the one way, the source. For in Him is all life, all health, all mind, all knowledge and immortality to the soul-mind itself.   3492-1

For how does one cleanse the mind? By the pouring out, the forgetting, the laying aside of those things that easily beset and *filling* same with pure, fresh water that is of the eternal life, that is of the eternal goodness as may be found in Him who *is* the light, the way, the truth, the vine, the bread of life and the water of life. These things are those influences that purify. . .   1620-1

Depend more upon the intuitive forces from within and not harken so much to that of outside influences but learn to listen to that still small voice from within, remembering the lesson as was given, not in the storm, the lightning, nor in any of the loud noises as are made to attract man, but rather in the still small voice from within does the impelling influence come to life in

...individual that gives for that which must be the basis of human endeavor; for without the ability to constantly hold before self the ideal as is attempted to be accomplished, man becomes one as adrift, pulled hither and yon by the various calls and cries of those who would give of this world's pleasure in fame, fortune, or whatnot. Let these be the outcome of a life spent in listening to the Divine from within, and not the purpose of the life.

239-1

This to some would appear an old, old, soul; yet all souls are as one—they were all of the same; for soul is eternal.

2542-1

An experience, then, is not only a happening, but what is the reaction in your own mind? What does it do to you to make your life, your habits, your relationships to others of a more helpful nature, with a more hopeful attitude?

These are the criterions for every individual's experience—sincerity of purpose, of desire; putting the whole law into effect in the activities—which is to love the Lord thy God with all thy heart, thy mind, thy body, and thy neighbor as thyself.

This is the whole law. All the other things given or written are only the interpreting of same.

Then what does such a proclaiming preclude? From what basis is the reasoning drawn? What is the purpose of an individual experience of an entity or soul into the earth at any given period?

These answered then give a background for the interpreting of *why*.

1567-2

Then, when ye abide in His presence, though there may come the trials of every kind, though the tears may flow from the breaking up of the carnal forces within self, the spirit is made glad. . .

262-33

Keep it [your soul] then in patience, in love, in gentleness, in kindness. . .For these are indeed the fruits of the spirit …And remember, a kindness sometimes consists in denying as well as granting those activities in associations with thy fellow man.   5322-1

They who would gain the greater will suffer the more. Those who would attain to a more perfect understanding of the true relationships of an individual to creative forces and using of same constructively, recognize the unfoldment of the mind through the experience.
                                                      5242-1

For, as has been indicated from the innate experience as well as from the longings within, a home—*home*—with all its deeper, inner meanings, is a portion of the entity's desire; to know, to experience, to have the "feel" of, to have the surroundings of that implied by the word *home!* Is it any wonder then that in all of thy meditation, Ohm—O-h-m-mmmmm has ever been, is ever a

portion of that which raises self to the
highest influence and the highest
vibrations throughout its whole being
that may be experienced by the entity?

1286-1

All souls were created in the
beginning, and are finding their way
back to whence they came.   3744-4

First know in self in what thou hast
believed, then set that as the ideal. . .
And when the darker days come, and
when the shadows come, that would
make thee afraid, turn within and have
a good time at scaring the bogies away
from those that would fear, that would
doubt.   815-2

For mind is the builder and that which
we think upon may become crimes or
miracles. For thoughts are things and
as their currents run through the
environs of an entity's experience these
become barriers or stepping-stones,
dependent upon the manner in which

these are laid, as it were. For as the mental dwells upon these thoughts, so does it give strength, power to things that do not appear. And thus does indeed there become that as is so oft given, that faith *is* the evidence of things not seen.   906-3

One that fills the mind, the very being, with an expectancy of God will see His movement, His manifestation, in the wind, the sun, the earth, the flowers, the inhabitants of the earth; and so as is builded in the body, is it to gratify just an appetite, or is it taken to fulfill an office that will the better make, the better magnify, that the body, the mind, the soul, has chosen to stand for? and it will not matter so much what, where, or when—but knowing that it is consistent with that—that is desired to be accomplished through that body! 341-31

Q-5. Please explain for me what is meant by "soul-mate"...

A-5. Those of any sect or group where there is the answering of one to another;

as would be the tongue to the groove, the tenon to the mortise; or in any such where they are a complement one of another—that is what is meant by "soul-mate." Not that as from physical attraction, but from the mental and spiritual help. 1556-2

Q-9. Am I an old or a young soul in evolutionary growth?

A-9. All souls are from one. It is the application that has grown to be that which is termed old or young soul. For all souls were created in the one. The entity has applied self, the entity has kept self close in contact with many who have through the awareness of the oneness of God's purpose with man been attempting to bring him to that awareness; and hence an "old" soul in service. 1770-2

Q-5. Why is it difficult for me to remember?

A-5. It isn't difficult! It's rather trained in self to forget! See the differentiation between forgetting and

14

remembering is *memory* in the exercising of the inner self as related to thought. To acknowledge that the memory is poor, is to say you don't think much! The forgetting is to say that the thought becomes self-centered, for memory is thought—even as thought is memory, brought to the forefront by the association of ideas.

69-2

And as He has given, "In all thy getting, my son, get understanding." That is putting proper emphasis in the proper places, and do not become sidetracked by things that would pertain to material or spiritual alone, or things of the body or things of the heavenly force. For you grow to heaven, you don't go to heaven. It is within thine own conscience that ye grow there. For there first must come peace and harmony within thy purpose, thy ideal, thy hopes, thy desires. Thy wishes even must be in harmony with thy ideal if you would make the experience in the earth of value to thee.   3409-1

On Choice and Will

. . .there is no urge in the astrological, in the vocational, in the hereditary or the environmental—which surpasses the will or determination of an entity. . . it is true there is nothing in heaven or hell that may separate the entity from the knowledge or from the love of the Creative Force, called God—but self.

5023-2

Q-8. If a soul fails to improve itself, what becomes of it?

A-8. That's why the reincarnation, why it reincarnates; that it may have the opportunity. Can the will of man continue to defy its Maker?   826-8

When fear of the future occurs, or fear of the past, or fear of what others will say—put all such away with this prayer—not merely by mouth, not merely by thought, but in body, in mind and in soul say: *"Here am I, Lord— Thine! Keep me in the way THOU would have me go, rather than in that I might choose."*

2540-1

And remember, *every* experience is a conditional one. For, choice must be made daily.

2034-1

Yes, thy Lord, thy God, showeth thee this day by day in His dealings with thy fellow man, to show those promises that have been made sure in the experiences of those that seek. For He giveth good and evil unto all, and ye choose through the *will* thy relationships—as to whether they shall be for self-exaltation, self-glorification, self-indulgence, self-gratification, or for the love of life, of truth, of hope, of honor, of virtue, of patience, of brotherly love. Ye yourselves show forth these in the manners, the ways ye deal with thy fellow man!

254-91

And each individual has the choice, which no one has the *right* to supersede—even God does not!

254-102

Where is thine *own* will? One with
His, or to the glorifying of thine own
desires—thine own selfish interests?

262-42

Any choice made by an individual is
to be worked *at.*   930-2

Think never that the opportunities
have passed; for ever is there set before
thee a choice to make, and has always
been given, *"Today* is the acceptable
year, the acceptable day of the Lord!" It
is never too late to begin even in an
experience; for Life in its experience is
a continued, a continuous effort—in
making, in starting, the associations
which bring what has ever been given
as the way whereby man may justify
himself before the throne of grace in a
material world: "Inasmuch as ye do it
unto the least of these, my little ones, ye
do it unto me."   909-1

Study to know thy self in relationship
to that ye choose as thy ideal. And let

that ideal be set in Him, who is the way, the truth and the light.

This does not mean becoming goody-goody, no—far from it! Be able to look *every man* in the face and tell him to go to hell—but *live* as He did, the lowly Nazarene!

2869-1

Q-2. What is meant by the children of light. . .?

A-2. They that choose to be guided by His will and do not, through themselves, attempt to manifest self rather than the will of the Father.

In the beginning was the word, and the word was God. He said, Let there be *light*—and there was light. Like begets like. It *is* both cause and effect, and they that choose some other way become the children of darkness; and they are these: Envying, strife, hate; and the children of these are sedition, rebellion, and the like.

The children of light first love, for "Though I may have the gift of prophecy, though I may speak in

unknown tongues, though I give my
body to be burned and have not the
spirit of the Son of man, the Christ
Consciousness, the Christ Spirit, I am
nothing." For, the children of light
know Him; He calleth each by name.

262-46

In the application of self as towards
will's influence: This the factor through
which one develops or retards in the
earthly experience.   97-2

With the arising of rebellious forces
...the body has assumed the attitude: "I
will break over this time, and next time
I won't. I will eat this because it pleases
me at the present. I will take this, for I
don't want to suffer right now, and next
time I won't." This has been done until
self loses such holds *on* self as to
become in a manner the slave to self's
own *indulgences,* in mental, physical
and material things!

These conditions, then, require that
there be made by self a definite stand to

be taken; that is: "If there is given me a definite program to follow I will—I *will*—I WILL adhere to it, no matter *what* I may suffer mentally or physically! I will *trust* in the *divine* forces innate. . .within my inner self for the *strength* to ENDURE, for the ability to say NO—when I should!"   911-7

Follow in that way that leads to the perfect understanding in Him, the giver of all good and perfect gifts, living as the ensample of manifested conditions exemplified in the body before a material world.

Be not faint hearted, nor overanxious, in the development, for the will of Him, the giver, must be made the will of man.

137-7

Yet the choice of that form which any of these shall take is ever dependent upon the *will*, that heritage from the Father that makes for every soul's development—whether as a companion for those environs of the celestial form

or whether the terrestrial or the earth
that must find its way. For the will of
self is as of the Father; He hath not
willed that any soul should perish but
hath with each temptation, with each
trial prepared a way of escape; making
as the bridge the Cross, over which each
soul may find the glory of its Lord and
of that to which it has sought to attain.

1246-2

*Q-6. What is the difference between
the desire of the heart and the desire of
the will?. . .*

A-6. Only in Him. In speaking of the
heart and of the will, analyze for the
moment as to what they represent in
thine own experience. The heart is
ordinarily considered the seat of life in
the physical, while the will as a
motivative factor in the mental and
spiritual realm. To be sure, these may
be made one. But how? In that the will of
self and the desire of the heart are
selfless in the Christ Consciousness.
Even as He gave in the shadow of the

day when the Cross loomed before Him
on Calvary, when the desire of the heart
and the will of self were made one.
Indeed, as He gave, the flesh is weak,
the spirit is willing...For, the soul is in
Him; yet, as the promise in the Christ is,
the soul shall be free in Him through
that love, through that manner of
making the desire and the will one in
the Father as did He in Gethsemane.

                                          262-64

Yet as we look into the infinity of
space and time we realize there is then
that force, that influence also that is
aware of the needs, and there is also that
will, that choice given to the souls of
men that they may be used, that they
may be one, that they may apply same
in their own feeble, weak ways perhaps;
yet that comes to mean, comes to
signify, comes to manifest in the lives
of those that have lost their way, that
very influence ye seek in the knowledge
of God.

For until ye become as a savior, as a

help to some soul that has lost hope, lost
its way, ye do not fully comprehend the
God within, the God without.   1158-14

. . .if thou art centered in Him, then be
not afraid! Yea, He has walked the
streets with the rabble and has seen the
flowing of the blessings that may come
through making self humble! Yea, in
the face and in the power of those that
might save the body, He gave: "There *is*
no power save that Creative Force we
call God may give," that the soul may be
raised, may be washed, may be white,
may be cleansed that it may be in the
presence of the Maker Himself! Art
thou choosing this way?   707-1

In the first was given man and mind to
subdue the earth in every element. As
given, again all manner of animal in the
earth, in the air, under the sea, has been
tamed of man, yet the man himself has
not reached that wherein he may
perfectly control himself, save making

the will one with the Creator, as man
makes the will of the animal one with
his. The control then in trained animals
being the projection in man. 900-31

For ever, day by day, is there a choice
to be made by each soul. One may lead to
happiness, joy; the other to confusion,
to disturbing forces, to evil and to self-
condemnation.

But the *will* is of self, else ye would
not indeed be the child of the Creative
and Living Force or God that ye are; but
as an automaton.

Then exercise thyself, and bring that
to pass in thy experience that will
create for *thee* the environ of helpful
hopefulness in the experience day by
day. 1538-1

Blessed, then, are they that make
their wills one in accord with Him, as
they seek to know, "Love, what would
Thou have me do!" 254-68

And the abilities are here to accomplish whatever the entity would choose to set its mind to, so long as the entity trusts not in the might of self, but in His grace, His power, His might. Be mindful ever of that, in thy understanding in thy own wisdom, much may be accomplished; but be rather thou the channel through which He, God, the Father, may manifest His power—in whatever may be the chosen activity of the entity.   3183-1

Then, do not count any condition lost. Rather make each the stepping-stone to higher things, remembering that God does not allow us to be tempted beyond that we are able to bear and comprehend, if we will but make our wills one with His.   900-44

If the experiences are ever used for self-indulgence, self-aggrandizement, self-exaltation, each entity does so to its *own* undoing, or creates for self that as

has been termed or called karma—and
must be met. And in meeting every
error, in meeting every trial, in meeting
every temptation—whether these be
mental or really physical experiences—
the manner and purpose and approach
to same should be ever in that attitude,
"Not my will but Thine, O God, be done
in and through me."   1224-1

For we *can,* as God, say Yea to this,
Nay to that; we *can* order this or the
other in our experience, by the very
gifts that have been given or appointed
unto our keeping. For we are indeed as
laborers, co-laborers in the vineyard of
the Lord—or of they that are fearful of
His coming.

And we choose each day *whom* we
will serve! And by the records in time
and space, as we have moved through
the realms of His kingdom, we have left
our mark upon same.   1567-2

For, no soul or entity enters without

opportunities. And the choice is ever
latent within self and the power, the
ability to do things, be things, to accept
things, is with the entity.   3226-1

Then all of these influences astrological (as known or called) from
without, bear witness—or *are* as innate
influences upon our activity, our
sojourn through any given experience.
Not because we were born with the sun
in this sign or that, nor because Jupiter
or Mercury or Saturn or Uranus or Mars
was rising or setting, but rather:

Because we were made for the
purpose of being companions with
Him, a little lower than the angels who
behold His face ever, yet as heirs, as
joint heirs with Him who *is* the Savior,
the Way, then we have brought these
about *because* of our activities through
our *experiences* in those realms! Hence
they bear witness by being *in* certain
positions—because of our activity, our
sojourn in those environs, in relationships to the universal forces of activity.

Hence they bear witness of certain urges in us, not beyond our will but controlled by our will!   1567-2

In the abilities, then—as is seen— *much* may be attained in the present experience. . .yet forget not that self must be kept aright, for through the will much may be gained or much may be lost.   37-1

All are in that position of being *able* to be used, if they will but recognize their opportunities day by day in their *choices* of dealings with their fellow men.

What is the choice? That as creates love, hope, faith, patience, kindness, gentleness in the experience. . .   1992-1

Know in self, first this: Thou art body, mind and soul, a three-dimensional individual in a three-dimensional consciousness. Hence ye find the Godhead, to a consciousness of an individual in the earth plane, is three

dimensions: Father, Son and Holy
Spirit. Each are individual, and yet they
are one. So with the body-conscious-
ness: the body, the mind and the soul.
Each have their attributes, each have
their limitations, save the soul.
Nothing may separate the soul from its
source save the will of self.   5089-3

There is today, every day, set before
thee good and evil, life and death—
choose thou. For only self can separate
you from the love of the Father. For it
should be manifested to thee that thou
art conscious in a living world, aware of
suffering, of sorrow, of joy, of pleasure.
These, to be sure, are the price one pays
for having will, knowledge. But let that
knowledge be spent in a way and
manner to help others. For as ye do to
thy fellow man ye do to thy Maker.

3581-1

Hence, will is given to man as he
comes into this manifested form that we

see in material forces, for the choice.

262-52

Then, when these are weighed, choose
thou. For, as has ever been, there is no
influence that may supersede the will of
man; for such are the gifts unto the sons
of men that they may make their souls
such as to be the companionship with
the All-Wise, All-Creative Forces, or
separate from them. For, there is no
impelling force other than that, "If ye
will be my people, I will be your God." It
is always thus.   440-16

Then—in correcting the entity—*do
not* ever break the entity's will! *Reason*
with the entity, for the mental ability
and aspects will incline to make the
entity become stubborn, if there is the
attempt to force or to cause the entity to
act in any direction or manner "just
because." Tell [the entity] why!   2308-1

But if ye are attempting to have thy
physical body doing just as it pleases,

thy mental body controlled by, "What will other people say?" and thy spiritual body and mind shelved only for good occasions for the good impression that you may make occasionally, there cannot be other than confusion.   1537-1

Each one who has a soul has a psychic power; but remember, brother, there are no shortcuts to God! You are there—but self must be eliminated.   5392-1

Thus ye may find in thy mental and spiritual self, ye can make thyself just as happy or just as miserable as ye like. How miserable do ye want to be? 2995-3

On Application

. . .there are no shortcuts to knowledge, to wisdom, to understanding—
these must be lived, must be experienced
by each and every soul.   830-2

Nothing grows, nothing remains
alone unless dead. A mind, a body that
sits alone and considers the outside and
never turning that within to the out, nor
that without from within, soon finds
drosses setting up in the system; for
development is change. Change is the
activity of knowledge from within.
Learn to *live!* Then there *is* no death,
save the transition, when desired. . .
                                 900-465

There is progress whether ye are
going forward or backward! The thing
is to move!   3027-2

This is the first lesson ye should
learn: There is so much good in the
worst of us, and so much bad in the best

of us, it doesn't behoove any of us to speak evil [of] the rest of us. This is a universal law, and until one begins to make application of same, one may not go very far in spiritual or soul development.   3063-1

And oh that all would realize, come to the consciousness that what we are—in any given experience, or time—is the combined result of what we have done about the ideals that we have set! 1549-1

Life is, in all its manifestations in every animate force, creative force in action; and is the love of expression—or expressing that life; truth becoming a result of life's love expressed. For, these are but names—unless experienced in the consciousness of each soul.
                    262-46

The way of the Cross is not easy, yet it is the tuneful, the rhythmic, the beautiful, the lovely way.   1089-6

You only fail if you quit trying. The
trying is oft counted for righteousness.
Remember as He has given, "I do not
condemn thee." Go be patient, be kind,
and the Lord be with thee!   3292-1

Then as ye have held, as ye have
applied that ye have gained, so does the
ability come to be of that help, that aid to
those who are stumbling—some
blindly, some gropingly, some discouraged, some overanxious, some
overzealous of their own peculiar twist
or turn; yet all seeking—seeking the
light.

But He is the light, as ye have seen in
thine experience—yea in thine experiences through the earth ye, too, have
seen the light and lost thy way. And
even as He put on flesh that He, too,
might know the ways of the flesh, of the
desires, of the urges that have wrought
in the experiences of men that
blindness of self-glory, self-indulgence
or self-aggrandizement that has led

many astray, even with the forces of
Divine at times working through them.

For the Spirit *is* willing, the flesh is
weak. And the strength, the influence,
the force and power, is by that trust, that
faith in Him. . .

1301-1

. . .all that ye may know of good must
first be within self. All ye may know of
God must be manifested through
thyself. To hear of Him is not to know.
To apply and live and be *is* to know!

2936-2

Man's destiny lies within his
individual grasp, doth he take hold
upon those laws, those self-evident
truths. Applying them in his relationships one to another there may come the
knowledge that He walketh and talketh
with those who would, who do, exalt and
glorify His name in the earth. . .

He was in the beginning, He is the
end. And as ye walk in the light of His
promise, of His words, ye may know the

way to go. For His light shineth in the
darkness and maketh the paths straight
for those that seek His face.   2454-4

All knowledge is to be used in the
manner that will give help and
assistance to others, and the desire is
that the laws of the Creator be
manifested in the physical world. 254-17

Acting as if it had not been; disregard-
ing as if it were not. Not animosity, for
this only breeds strife; not anger, for
this will only produce mentally and
physically the disturbances, that
become as physical reactions that
prevent meeting every phase of the
experience, whether in the good, the
hope, the help ye mete to others, or in
keeping self...unspotted from the cares
of the world.   1402-2

Know that the purpose for which each
soul enters a material experience is

that it may be as a light unto others; not
as one boastful of self or of self's
abilities in any phase of the experience,
whether mental or material, but living,
being in spirit that which *is* ideal and
not idealistic alone, nor the unattainable.

For, as He hath given—if ye would
know the Spirit, or God, search for Him;
for happily ye will find Him.

Thus—in that consciousness of daily
living and being that which is in
keeping with the ideal—life and its
problems become not a burden, but
opportunities—for the greater expressions and expansions of self in knowing
that as ye sow daily the fruit of the spirit
ye need not worry nor fret thyself as to
its growth. God giveth the increase.
Hence be not weary in well-doing. 641-6

Q-4. How may the doubt be prevented?
A-4. By the application of that thou
knowest to do today, putting the trust in
Him, *making* the *personal* application
of that thou knowest to do in *His* name.
524-2

What ye *find* to do, with willing hands
DO ye.   254-87

There is that access, then, that way to
the Throne of grace, of mercy, of peace,
of understanding, within thine own self.
For He hath promised to meet thee in
thine own temple, in thine own body,
through thine own mind. . .And then
enter into the holy of holies within thine
own consciousness; turn within; see
what has prompted thee, and He has
promised to meet thee there. And there
shall it be *told* thee from within the
steps thou shalt take day by day, step by
step. Not that some great exploit, some
great manner of change should come
within thine body, thine mind, but line
upon line, precept upon precept, here a
little, there a little. For it is, as He has
given, not the knowledge alone but the
practical application—in thine daily
experience with thy fellow man—that
counts.   922-1

. . .not only proclaim or announce a belief in the Divine, and to promise to dedicate self to same, but the entity must *consistently* live such. And the test, the proof of same, is long-suffering. This does not mean suffering of self and not grumbling about it. Rather, though you be persecuted, unkindly spoken of, taken advantage of by others, you do not attempt to fight back or to do spiteful things; that you be patient—first with self, then with others; again that you not only be passive in your relationships with others but active, being kindly, affectionate one to the other; remembering, as He has said, "Inasmuch as ye do it unto the least, ye do it unto me." As oft as you contribute, then, to the welfare of those less fortunate, visit the fatherless and the widows in their affliction, visit those imprisoned—rightly or wrongly— you do it to your Maker. For *truth* shall indeed make you free, even though you be bound in the chains of those things that have brought errors, or the result of errors, in your own experience.   3121-1

It is the "try" that is the more often counted as righteousness, and *not* the success or failure. Failure to anyone should be as a stepping-stone and not as a millstone.   931-1

For know that each soul constantly meets its own self. No problem may be run away from. *Meet* it NOW!   1204-3

It is not *what* one says that counts, but what one *is!*   524-2

It is not the knowledge, then, but what one does with one's abilities, one's opportunities in relationships to others, that makes for the development or retardment of that individual.

For life in its manifestations through which the soul of an entity or body may manifest *is* purposeful, and that the individual, the soul may find its way through the vicissitudes of experience in materiality, that it may know its God.

For He manifested in flesh that the evil forces, as manifest in the relationships of individuals as one to another, may be eradicated from the experiences of man.   1293-1

As He has given, and as has been presented again and again, not in times nor seasons, not in new moons nor in any place, but *every* day, *every* hour we show forth His love in a manner that makes for the knowledge of all contacting us that He walks with us, that He is our friend.   262-36

As to how—though ye may not of thyself, put the burden on Him and it becomes light. But *act* in the manner as He did, not resenting any. For remember, as He said to that one who had promised that though all might forsake Him, he never would, yet in the same hour denied that he ever knew Him— "When thou art converted, strengthen

thy brethren." Thus may it be given to
thee—if ye put that resentment away, if
ye put that doubt and that fear upon
Him, He will cast it out; but thee,
strengthen thy brethren. Teach, preach,
talk to others, as to how they should
leave such at the cross and *only*
magnify, manifest, *know* that they need
not attempt to justify themselves. For
all the justification is in Him. We need
then only to *glorify* that love, that hope,
that understanding which He brings to
each soul that seeks His face.   2600-2

Then, *we* would give that not only
must the body-mind turn to the
spiritual promises that are a part of its
mental and spiritual self, but the
environment must be changed; so that
the spiritual promises may be put to
active service and work to replace the
habits with the habits of doing *good,*
doing right, doing justice, being
merciful.   1427-1

. . .to meet the disturbing factors with
as much joyousness as if they were

bringing pleasure in the material sight
will alter...much in the heart and mind
of the seeker. For that which is, is a
result of the thinking of individuals as
related one to another.   610-1

For this entity should comprehend
and *know,* and *never* forget, that life and
its experiences are only what one puts
into same! And unless the activities, the
thoughts are *continuously* constructive, and the experience well-balanced,
the entity *cannot, will* not fulfill the
purpose for which it came into the
present experience.   1537-1

To continue to condemn only brings
condemnation, then, for self. This does
not mean that self's activity should be
passive, but rather being constant in
prayer—knowing and taking—knowing and understanding that he that is
faithful is not given a burden beyond
that he is able to bear, if he will put the
burden upon Him that has given the

promise, "I will be *with* thee; there shall not come that which shall harm thee, if thou will but put thy trust, thy faith in me."

Know that only in Him, who may bring peace and harmony by or through the contacts—the thoughts of self in relationship to the whole—may there be brought better relationships.

First make an analysis of self, of self's relationships, of the impelling influences that cause others to act in their manners in the present.

Do not condemn self; do not condemn another; but leave the activities that would bring about condemnation rather in His hands, who requireth at the hands of all, that there be meted, "As ye would that should be done to thee, do ye even so to thy fellow man!" 290-1

Thoughts
and
Feelings

For, as has been given, it is not all of
life to live, nor yet all of death to die. For
life and death are one, and only those
who will consider the experience as one
may come to understand or comprehend what peace indeed means.   1977-1

Be happy—be in the attitude of ever
being helpful to others. These will bring
that peace within that is the promise
from Him.   1968-7

If it is held. . .as a cross, it will remain
as one. . .with individuals where there
[are] in their experiences crosses to
bear, hardships or surroundings that to
them are overpowering, overwhelm-
ing, by slights, slurs, and fancies of the
inactivity of a coordinating force. If
these are held continually as crosses, or
as things to be overcome, then they will
remain as crosses. But if they are to be
met with the spirit of truth and right in
their own selves, they should create *joy*;
for that is what will be built.   552-2

Count thy hardships, thy troubles, even thy disappointments, rather as stepping-stones to know His way better. 262-83

. . .man looketh upon the outward appearance, God looketh upon the heart. The gain or retardment is according to the purpose, the cause for such activities being a part of an entity's experience. 2905-3

For many an individual entity, those things that are of sorrow are the greater helps for unfoldment. . . 3209-2

Change the body thoughts—we will change the effect upon those activities in the throat, in the eyes, in the ears, and the body forces. . .Remember the law— and the law of the Lord is perfect, in body, in mind, in spirit. And as laws of the physical, of the mental, of the spiritual are kept in unison of purpose,

a more perfect balance is kept in the
body.   3246-2

. . .happiness is love of something
outside of self! It may never be obtained,
may never be known by loving only
things within self or self's own domain!
281-30

Never so act, in *any* manner, in any
inclination, that there may ever be an
experience of regret within self. Let the
moves and the discourteousness, the
unkindness, all come from the other.
Better to be abased. . .and have the peace
within!. . .act ever in the way ye would
like to be acted toward. No matter *what*
others say or even *do*, do as ye would be
done by; and then the peace that has
been promised is *indeed* thine own.
1183-3

Thus no wonder confusion comes,
unless there is held to the one mighty
purpose—*Love Divine* that so over-
shadows all else as to be that alone that

makes an experience in the earth
worthwhile. . .   1402-1

Learn this lesson well of the spiritual
truth: Criticize not unless ye wish to be
criticized. For with what measure ye
mete it is measured to thee again. It may
not be in the same way, but ye cannot
even *think* bad of another without it
affecting thee in a manner of a
destructive nature.
Think *well* of others and if ye *cannot*
speak well of them don't speak! but
don't think it either!   2936-2

For to hold grudges, to hold malice, to
hold those things that create or bring
contention, only builds the barrier to
prevent thy *own* inner self enjoying
peace and contentment.   1608-1

Is there really the desire to know love,
or to know the experience of someone

having an emotion over self? Is it a
desire to be itself expended in doing that
which may be helpful or constructive?
This *can* be done, but it will require the
losing of self, as has been indicated, *in*
service for others.

...But arise to that consciousness that
if ye would have life, if ye would have
friends, if ye would have love, these
things ye must expend. For only that ye
give away do ye possess.   1786-2

Love goes far beyond what you call
the grave.   5756-14

For perfect love casteth out fear, and
fear can only be from the material
things that soon must fade away.

And thus hold to the higher thought of
eternity. For life is a *continual*
experience.   1175-1

...for in suffering *strength* is gained,
even as the wind bloweth where it

listeth—one heareth the sound thereof
and knoweth not whither it cometh nor
whence it goeth, yet that is as of the
thought and intent in the individual
characterization of self—that out of
those forces comes that same in an
individual or entity's being.   5528-1

For until ye are willing to *lose* thyself
in service, ye may not indeed know that
peace which He has promised to give—
to all.   1599-1

. . .that contentment that can only
come with the knowledge of *His* peace
abiding ever with thee; for with *His*
peace there comes contentment, no
matter what may be the vicissitudes of
life, whether in trials as of the mental
surroundings, whether in the trials as
of material conditions or positions,
there can come—with that peace—that
contentment of heart *and* mind, that He
is in His holy temple and all is well with
those who have made Him the ideal. . .
     451-2

. . .only music may span that space
between the finite and the infinite
...music may be the means of arousing
and awakening the best of hope, the best
of desire, the best in the heart and soul
of those who will and do listen. Is not
music the universal language, both for
those who would give praise and those
who are sorry in their hearts and souls?
Is it not a means, a manner of universal
expression? Thus, may the greater
hope come.   2156-1

For hope and faith are living—
living—things! Thus hope springs
anew with the growth and the knowledge and the understanding of the light
on the way, and that life indeed is an
eternal expression of the love of the
Father; and that as it gives the
expression through the individuality of
each and every soul as it comes in
material manifestation by the weak-
nesses, we find the strength in the
Lord—and in the glories ever in His

beauteous purpose with each soul; that purpose that ye might be the companions, one with Him. 1504-1

. . .to bring hope, to bring cheer, to bring joy, yea to bring a smile again to those whose face and heart are bathed in tears and in woe, is making that divine love *shine—shine—*in thy own soul. Then *smile,* be joyous, be glad! For the day of the Lord is at hand. 987-4

But to know that ye spoke unkindly and suffered for it, and in the present may correct it by being righteous—*that* is worthwhile! 5753-2

If the problems of the experience today, now, are taken as an expectancy for the unusual and that which is to be creative and hopeful and helpful, life becomes rather the creative song of the joyous worker.

If the same problems become

humdrum, something to be fought through, something to be questioned as to their purpose, their activity, their usefulness in the experience, then the life becomes rather as a drone, as of one drudging, coming through toil, and with only turmoil and a vision unclaimed, unactive in its associations with the general conditions of the day.

1968-5

Do not hold resentment. Do not get so mad at times when things are a little wrong. Remember that others have as much right to their opinions as self, but that there *is* a level from which all may work together for good.

Smile always—and *live* the smile!

1819-1

Happiness, then, is not a thing set apart from self, but the conditions with which one approaches that in hand to be *done!* For when one considers that the position of self is hard to bear, is not as is desired, the desire of the heart often maketh one *afraid*—unless that desire is ever in that attitude of "*Use me,* O God, as I am," for the I AM is ready, willing, to make *my* will *one* with *Thy will*—"Though He slay me, though He bruise me in mine own selfish or unseen ways; yet will I trust Him day by day," and He will *not* forsake thee; neither will He allow thee to be afraid; for He will raise thee up, and He understands all the hardships, the *little* things, the separations, the variations in the surroundings—but *trust* Him! 5563-1

Remember, the soft word turns away wrath, and it brings joy, the kind word as ye have found in thine own experience oft has made the day much brighter for thee. Make many days brighter for others and in making them more and more in attune with love, patience, long-suffering, gentleness and kindness, ye will make for thyself a surety in those things that take hold on peace, harmony and joy. These should be a part of thine experience ever. 5098-1

That primarily needed is patience, persistence and consistence.

Then we would define for the entity what we mean by the entity having patience—in an active, positive manner and not merely as a passive thing.

Taking or enduring hardships, or censure, or idiosyncrasies of others, is not necessarily patience at all. It may become merely that of being a drudge not only to self but an outlet of expression from others that may never be quite satisfying because there is no resistance.

Passive patience, to be sure, has its place; but consider patience rather from the precepts of God's relationship to man: Love unbounded is patience. Love manifested is patience. Endurance at times is patience, consistence ever is patience.   3161-1

Who gains by being forgiven and by forgiving? The one that forgives is lord even of him that he forgives.   585-2

So be ye then as His children—those

that show joy and gladness in the lives, the experiences, the hearts, the minds of those ye meet day by day; thus becoming indeed brethren with Him, in that He gave Himself as a ransom for all, that whosoever will may take *their* cross and *through* Him know the joy of entering into that realm of replacing jealousy and hate and selfishness with love and with joy and with gladness.

Be ye glad. Be ye joyous when those things come to be thy lot that should or would disturb the material-minded. Like Him, look up, lift up thy heart, thy mind unto the Giver of all good and perfect gifts; and cry aloud even as He, "My God, my God! Be Thou near unto me!"

In this, as ye raise then thy voice to Him, ye may be sure He will answer, "Here am I—be not afraid. For as the Father hath sent me, so come I into thy heart and life to bring gladness, that there may be life more abundant in thy experience."

Then, be ye *glad* in Him. 5749-10

Hence again might that injunction be given the entity not to be too easily discouraged. Brace up! *Know* in what ye have believed and do believe, but know *who* is also the *author* of such. For life *is* real, life *is* earnest, and the grave is *not* the goal!   1792-2

Be *glad* you have the opportunity to be alive at this time, and to be a part of that preparation for the coming influences of a spiritual nature that *must* rule the world. These are indicated, and these are part of thy experience. Be happy of it, and give thanks daily for it.   2376-3

. . .each soul has a mission in the earth, and is in expression a manifestation of the thought of God, of the First Cause. Thus all stand upon an equal basis before Him.

Then, ye have no right to condemn self or to judge others.

Let all be done rather, then, as an appreciation of the love, the thought as may be expressed in appreciation to that Creative Force called God.

And the greater lessons ~~may be~~ learned from His manifested activity in the earth through Christ Jesus.   2683-1

...don't get mad and don't cuss a body out mentally or in voice. This brings more poisons than may be created by even taking foods that aren't good.

470-37

Wherever Truth is made manifest it gives place to that which is heaven *for those that seek* and love truth!   262-87

To not know, but do the best as is known, felt, experienced in self, to him it is counted as righteousness.   1728-2

What separates ye from seeing the glory even of Him that walks with thee oft in the touch of a loving hand, in the voice of those that would comfort and cheer? For He, thy Christ, is oft with thee.

Doubt, fear, unbelief; fear that thou art not worthy!

Open thine eyes and behold the glory,

even of thy Christ present here, now, in
thy midst! even as He appeared to them
on that day!   5749-6

Then, to be able to remember the
sunset, to be able to remember a
beautiful conversation, a beautiful
deed, done where hope and faith were
created, to remember the smile of a
babe, the blush of a rose, the harmony of
a song—a bird's call; *these* are creative.
For if they are a part of thyself, they
bring you closer and closer to God.

1431-1

That there have been many problems
and many questionings is true; yet
when the entity has allowed or does
allow itself to meditate upon the
principles of the prompting which
come from its study, its application of
the law of the Lord which is manifested
in the precepts, the commandments, the
psalms and the promises of Jesus, little
has been the fear of what the man-force
has to offer as to disturbing factors in
the earth.

Then, as would be given, keep that faith. . .do not let those things which may not in the present be understood weary thy soul, but know that sometime, somewhere, you, too, will understand. Keep the faith.   5369-2

Keep to those purposes, those attitudes of helpful hopefulness; that the opportunities accorded may be used in service to others. Such an attitude kept in the mental forces will bring the *renewing* of the faith in the Divine, which *is* the heritage of every soul.

849-25

As has been indicated, a little more patient, a little more tolerant, a little more humble. But. . .not a tolerance that becomes timid—this would make rebellion in self. Not a patience that is not positive. Not humbleness that becomes morbid or lacking in beauty. For as orderliness is a part of thy being, so let consistency—as persistency—be a part of thy being.   1402-1

. . .they that would have cooperation *must* cooperate by the *giving* of self *to* that as is to be accomplished—whether in the bringing of light to others, bringing of strength, health, understanding, these are one *in* Him. . .

This is a natural consequence of self-service, self-sacrifice, self-*bewilderment,* in Him. Being the channel is cooperation. Being a blessing is it in action. In whatever *state* of being, meet that upon the basis of *their* position— and *lift* up, look up—and *this* is cooperation.   262-3

And when ye trust in Him, ye are sure—and need never be afraid of the material things. For, does He not feed the birds of the air? Does He not give the color to the lily, the incense to the violet? How much more is that as may be in His very presence, if ye apply self to become worthy of acceptance in His home.   3333-1

On Living
in
the Earth

Know the first principles: There is
good in all that is alive.   2537-1

The entity should keep close to all of
those things that have to do with
outdoor activities, for it is the best way
to keep yourself young—to stay close to
nature, close to those activities in every
form of exercise that breathes in the
deep ozone and the beauty of nature. For
you may breathe it into thine own soul,
as you would a sunset or a morning sun
rising. And see that sometimes—it's as
pretty as the sunset!   3374-1

. . .the church is within yourself and
not in any pope or preacher, or in any
building but in self! For thy body is
indeed the temple of the living God, and
the Christ becomes a personal companion in mind and in body; dependent
upon the personality and the individuality of the entity as it makes practical

application of the tenets and truths that
are expressed.   5125-1

For, from the desire of the heart the
mouth speaketh. From the meditations
of the soul the hands, the body, the mind,
find their manner of manifestation of
that which motivates same in material
expressions.   683-2

In materiality we find some advance
faster, some grow stronger, some
become weaklings. Until there is
redemption through the acceptance of
the law (or love of God, as manifested
through the Channel or the Way), there
can be little or no development in a
material or spiritual plane. But all must
pass under the rod, even as He—who
entered into materiality.   5749-3

Show due consideration as to how
much ye owe the world, rather than as to
how much the world owes you!

The world owes every individual *only* an opportunity to express itself and its idea of the Creative Forces—which will find expression in the manner we treat our fellow men.   2172-1

Know that what is *truly* thine *cannot* be taken away from thee. . .   2448-2

. . .peace must begin within self before there may be the activity or the application of self in such a manner as to bring peace in thy own household, in thine own heart, in thine own vicinity, in thine own state or nation.   3976-28

For know, the earth and all therein is the Lord's. All thine *own* is lent thee, not thine but *lent* thee. Keep it inviolate.
                                                           2622-1

Do not worry as to whether you are fat or thin. Worry rather as to whether you use your body, mentally and physically, as an expression of thy ideal.   308-8

The purpose in life, then, is not the gratifying of appetites nor of any selfish desires, but it is that the entity, the soul, may make the earth, where the entity finds its consciousness, a better place in which to live.   4047-2

Count it rather as an opportunity, a gift of a merciful Father, that there are the opportunities in the present for the sojourn in the material influences; that the advantages may be taken of opportunities that come into the experience, even through the hardships and disappointments that have arisen.
                    1709-3

. . .that we see manifested in the material plane is but a shadow of that in the spiritual plane.   5749-3

Perfection is not possible in a material body until you have entered at least some thirty times.   2982-2

...as the body may dedicate its life and
its abilities to a definite service, to the
Creative Forces, or God, there will be
healing forces brought to the body. This
requires, then, that the mental attitude
be such as to not only proclaim or
announce a belief in the Divine, and to
promise to dedicate self to same, but the
entity must *consistently* live such.

3121-1

Study more to understand that each at
all times stands in the presence of that
Power, that Force, that brings to each
the power of knowing self in a material
world. Each act, each thought of each
body adds to the bringing about of His
Kingdom in the earth, or adds to that
which prevents it from becoming
manifest in this material plane. .   911-6

For, know all power, all influence that
is of a creative nature is of the Father-
God a manifestation. Not as an
individual, not as a personality, but as
good, as love, as law, as long-suffering,

as patience, as brotherly love, as kindness, as gentleness; yet in all the beauties of nature—in the blush of the rose, in the baby's smile, in the song of the bird, in the ripple of the brook, in the wind, in the wave, in all of those influences or forces that bring to His creatures a consciousness of Life itself and its awareness and its activity in a material plane. 1276-1

. . .do not be afraid of giving self in a service—if the *ideal* is correct. If it is selfish motives, or for aggrandizement, or for obtaining a hold to be used in an underhand manner, *beware*. If it is that the glory of truth may be made manifest, *spend it all*—whether self, mind, body, or the worldly means— whether in labor or in the coin of the realm. 1957-1

For it is only in [love] that one becomes, in materiality, aware of the closeness of relationship to the Creative Forces or God. 1703-3

For Life and its expressions are one.
Each soul or entity will and does return,
or cycle, as does nature in its manifestations about man; thus leaving, making,
or presenting—as it were—those
infallible, indelible truths that it—
Life—is continuous. And though there
may be a few short years in this or that
experience, they are one; the soul, the
inner self being purified, being lifted
up, that it may be one with that first
cause, that first purpose for its coming
into existence.   938-1

Remember, healing—all healing
comes from within. Yet there is the
healing of the physical, there is the
healing of the mental, there is the
correct direction from the spirit.
Coordinate these and you'll be whole!
But to attempt to do a physical healing
through the mental conditions is the
misdirection of the spirit that prompts
same. . .

But when the law is coordinated in

spirit, in mind, in body, the entity is capable of fulfilling the purpose for which it enters a material or physical experience. 2528-2

For within the human body—living, not dead—*living* human forces—we find every element, every gas, every mineral, every influence that is outside of the organism itself. For indeed it is one with the whole. For it is not only a portion of, and equal to, and able to overcome or meet every influence within, but there is not the ability in the third dimensional force or influence to even imagine anything that isn't a part of the activity of a physical *living* organism! 470-22

Know that it is not all just to live—not all just to be good, but good *for* something; that ye may fulfill that purpose for which ye have entered this experience. 2030-1

...unless each soul entity...makes the world better, that corner or place of the world a little better, a little bit more hopeful, a little bit more patient, showing a little more of brotherly love, a little more of kindness, a little more of long-suffering—by the very words and deeds of the entity, the life is a failure; especially so far as growth is concerned. Though you gain the whole world, how little ye must think of thyself if ye lose the purpose for which the soul entered this particular sojourn!

3420-1

Meditate, oft. Separate thyself for a season from the cares of the world. Get close to nature and *learn* from the lowliest of that which manifests in nature, in the earth; in the birds, in the trees, in the grass, in the flowers, in the bees; that the life of each is a manifesting, is a song of glory to its Maker. And do thou *likewise!*   1089-3

Do not be overanxious about the material things. For the mental and the spiritual aspects and desires should be set in those directions whereunto it may be said in the experience of self, "I myself will be guided by the influences from the inner meditations, and that which is shown me from within." For to such the promises are sure. If ye will seek this way, there may come those experiences that will not only be of more harmonious nature in the affairs in material things, but will bring that contentment which comes from knowing within self that the way is being kept that leads to a greater understanding in the truths, in mental experiences of a body.   681-1

Know that ye are going through a period of testing. Remain true to all that has been committed to thee, and know that each day is an opportunity, and an experience. Speak a word for thy ideal. Not as to force an issue but ever constructive. Sow the seed of truth, the seed of the spirit. God will give the increase.   3245-1

Music should be a part of each soul's
development.   2780-3

All things having force or power in
the earth, in the heavens, in the sea, are
given that power from Him; that those
who seek may know Him the better. He
hath not willed, He hath not destined
that any soul should perish. In patience,
in persistency, in consistency of thy
manifestations of His love before and to
and of thy fellow man, ye become aware
that thy soul is a portion of the Creator,
that it is the gift of the Father *to thee*.
This is manifested in thine daily
experience. That portion of thy body
which is of the earth-earthy remains
with the earth, but that thou hast
glorified, that thou hast used as a
channel for the manifestations of His
Spirit—of thy soul in communion with
Him, *that* body will be raised with Him
in righteousness. That the physical
body becomes ensnared, entangled in
those things in the earth, through the
gratifying of those desires that are
fleshly alone, those that are carnal, is

manifested by the dis-ease, the corruption, the turmoil, the strife that arises within the experience of each soul in its *thoughtful* activities in the earth. 272-9

What one thinks continually, they become; what one cherishes in their heart and mind they make a part of the pulsation of their heart, through their own blood cells, and build in their own physical, that which its spirit and soul must feed upon and that with which it will be possessed, when it passes into the realm for which the other experiences of what it has gained here in the physical plane, must be used. 3744-4

. . .in thine own heart there comes those things that would make afraid. But fear is of the earth. The spirit of truth and righteousness casteth out fear. 397-1

For, the experience or sojourn in the earth is not chance, but the natural

spiritual and soul evolution of the
entity; that it may be aware of its
relationships to God—through its
relationships to its fellow men;
recognizing in each soul, as well as in
self, those possibilities, those opportunities, those duties, those obligations
that are a portion of each soul-entity's
manifesting in a material plane. 2271-1

For the material, at best, is only
temporal, or temporary, while that
which may be builded from spiritual
desire, spiritual purposes, is eternal.

1971-1

First—know as to what are the
purposes, the desires, the hopes. There
are in the present the problems that are
a part of the experience, but take things,
conditions and circumstances where
they are—not merely where you
wishfully think, hope or desire that
they are!

Meet the problems first, though, in the
spiritual; then the mental and the

material results will become more satisfactory. As the law has been and is a portion of the hopes—as the associations are still many of the problems of the moment—find the solution in the choices as in keeping with these:

Thou has seen the way of the Lord. Thou knowest it to be good. Depart not from same for the satisfying or the gratifying of material wishes or material desires. For, the law of the Lord is perfect; and they that seek to follow in His way shall not find themselves among those disturbed, nor among the children of want.   459-12

Hence as has been given, *know thyself,* in *whom* thou believest! Not of earthly, not of material things, but mental and spiritual—and *why!* And by keeping a record of self—not as a diary, but thy purposes, what you have thought, what you have desired, the good that you have done—we will find this will bring physical and mental reactions that will be in keeping with

the purposes for which each soul enters
a material manifestation.   830-3

In the care of self, selflessness is
great. But be more mindful of the little
niceties about self and you will find a
pride in self—not a false pride. But as
nature manifested in its Maker, it does
the best it can with what it has and looks
the most beautiful with what it has to do
with. Thy body, too, is indeed the temple
of the living God. Keep it beautiful. Be
mindful of the care of same, and you—
too—will think more of it. So will there
be more of the abilities to be conscious
of His presence meeting with thee in thy
temple; forget it not.   3179-1

Prayer is just as scientific as the
knife, in its individual field. Mechano-
therapy or mechanical treatments are
as effective in their individual fields,
and are of the same source as prayer—if
applied in the same manner, or *with* the
same sincerity.   1546-1

For all healing, mental or material, is attuning each atom of the body, each reflex of the brain forces, to the awareness of the Divine that lies within each atom, each cell of the body. 3384-2

Each entrance of an entity into a material experience is that it may better fit itself, through the application of an ideal in its experience, for a sojourn with that which is Creative—that influence or force in which all move and have their consciousness, their being. 1759-1

For these are trying times. And know that there is no one in authority that has not been raised to same by the grace of Creative Forces. Each then is being given (that is in authority) the opportunity for expressing those purposes in his relationships and dealings with the fellow man—for the very reason of his abilities as a leader.

Then do thou that thou knowest to be the constructive experience in thy field, and trouble not thy mind or heart as to others. For the very thought of there becoming turmoil is *opening* the way *for* turmoil.   816-10

"Fear not, I am with thee." This should be upon the mind, the heart; that there may be the renewing of the lifeflow in the *blood* of the body, that the organs thereof may be attuned to the spiritual. . .   1089-2

In the material associations, in the material connections, then, do with thy might what thy hand finds to do *today.* For sufficient unto the day is the good as well as the evil thereof. For as He hath given in thee that thou may be a channel, the representative, the agent— yea, the very representative in flesh of Him, then act in thine inner self, act in thine outward expression, as though thou wert (for thou art!) His child, and are heir to all the glories *here,* NOW, of His kingdom. *Not* in the future, not of the past! For in the eternal *now* is He *active* in thee.   683-2

On Self and Others

More individuals become so anxious about their own troubles, and yet helping others is the best way to rid yourself of your own troubles. For what is the pattern? He gave up heaven and entered physical being that ye might have access to the Father.   5081-1

For, while selflessness is the law, to belittle self is a form of selfishness and not selfless.   2803-2

For he that contributes only to his own welfare soon finds little to work for. He that contributes only to the welfare of others soon finds too much of others and has lost the appreciation of self, or of its ideals. . .

Know that the power or strength for any influence as related to the help of others must come from the universal source and not from self alone. For the individual may sow the seed, the Infinite must give the increase—it must do the multiplying. Man can detract, but he can add little to God's purpose in the earth save through the grace and mercy of God Himself.   3478-2

Learn first that lesson of cooperation. Become less and less selfish, and more and more selfless in Him. Be not afraid to be made fun of to become aware of His presence, that self may be a channel through which the glory of the Father may come unto men in a manner that all may know there is a glory, even an Israel, of the Lord.   262-29

Unless those activities among men are the aid for the greater number, rather than for the class or the few, they must eventually fail.   826-2

For the greater individual is the one who is the servant of all. And to conquer self is greater than taking many cities. For, here ye may find humbleness as against that which cries oft for expression, and the feeling of not being appreciated. Express it more in the greater amount of love upon those who

may be aided through thy effort. For,
remember, man looks upon the things
of the day but God looks upon the heart.
3253-2

Faults in others are first reflected in
self. When such conditions arise in the
experience of an entity, there should be
first those considerations of that in self
that has produced such a reflection, so
that the God shining through any
activity is lost sight of by self in the
fellow man; especially one that is
seeking for the spiritual activities in a
material plane, and he that would gain
the world and lose self's *own* soul has
lost all.   452-3

But the less one thinks of self's
opinions and the better listener one
becomes, greater may be the opportunities for being of help or benefit to
those about the entity.   2612-1

...to express love in thine activities to
thy neighbor is the greater service that

a soul may give in this mundane
sphere.   499-2

. . .what are friends? That in which
there may be the testing of our own
abilities, as to that application of truth
related to the Divine and to mental
reactions in relationship one to
another.   2772-5

If you would have friends, be friendly.
If you would even have fun, make fun
for someone else.

Read the comic papers; not as to
become sarcastic, no—but remember,
ever, even thy Master, Jesus, could
laugh in the face of the cross. Can ye
find a better example?   3440-2

Friendships are only the *renewing* of
former purposes, ideals.   2946-2

But do not put off today that which
will bring hope and help to the mind of
another. . .Those things that make for
the putting off become a joy never

fulfilled. Use, then, the experiences
from day to day as the basis, and these
will *grow under thine very effort;*
surprising even to self as to the joy that
comes from same, and gradually taking
shape to become a joy to self and
blessings to others.   877-9

Then what are you grumbling about
because you dislike your mother? She
dislikes you as much, but change this
into love. Be kind, be gentle, be patient,
be long-suffering, for if thy God was not
long-suffering with thee, what chance
would you have?   5081-1

But the entity should know there is
more to life than to live, and a success
must be one in which the entity may
grow in understanding and in knowledge. It must be one in which grace and
mercy and truth *have* been and *are* the
directing activities; else regrets, in the
home, in the associations, may be the
part of the entity's experience.

Keep self, then, well-balanced. Budget thy time more. . .

For he that makes material gains at the expense of home or of opportunities and obligations with his own family does so to his own undoing. 1901-1

TRY in thine own experience, each; that ye speak not for *one whole day* unkindly of any; that ye say not a harsh word to any, about any; and see what [such] a day would bring to you. . .

262-106

Be ye mindful that He of whom ye speak, when ye preach, giveth power to the words, only as ye practice it in thine own life. Ye may not expect to succeed in convincing thy brother that he should be patient or kind, or even hear thee, unless ye are patient and kind thyself. Don't preach one thing and practice another. For this is inconsistent, and inconsistency is sin, and be sure thy sins will find thee out. . .

Don't keep telling people what they ought to do, nor keep telling them what a great personage thou art, but so live that thy life is consistent with what the word speaketh. For, as ye may know, and should know, by this period, "Thou shalt love the Lord, thy God, with all thy heart and mind and body, and thy neighbor as thyself," is the whole gospel and as ye live it ye can preach it ...For whatsoever a man soweth, that he must also reap.   5275-1

Each soul. . .has a definite job to do. But ye alone may find and do that job.

2823-1

Make haste slowly, for one can easily become discouraged. One can become overenthusiastic. One can become in such a manner of policy as to let the little ends slip without proper consideration, as to their meaning with the whole undertaking.   2448-3

"For all that ye may ever kee
what you give away, and that
away is advice, counsel, manner of life
you live yourself." The manner in
which you treat your fellow man, your
patience, your brotherly love, your
kindness, your gentleness. That you
give away, that is all that ye may
possess in those other realms of
consciousness.   5259-1

Know thyself, then, to be as a
corpuscle, as a facet, as a characteristic,
as a love, in the body of God.   2533-7

For as in the manner ye treat thy
fellow man ye treat thy Maker. And ye
cannot do that which is questioning in
thine own heart and soul to thy
neighbor, to thy wife, to thy child,
without it bringing turmoil, without it
bringing discontent, without it bringing confusion. For these are the
children of confusion, questioning
thine own self.

Then, in what way, in what manner, where has the error been, how can the self find self?

Know first, the Lord thy God hath not tempted any soul, He hath not given any soul that that it may not meet. And He hath prepared a way of escape for each soul if it will but harken to that voice deep *within!* Not through some long-winded individual's sayings, not that there will not be those inclinations to say, "Well, this or that or the other makes little or no difference," but that which is the prompting of the inner conscience.   417-8

Know that a smile will rally many to thy cause, while a frown would drive all away.   2448-2

He who doubts that the best will come to him with doing of that which is correct is already defeated. Don't blame others for what has happened or may happen. Do right yourself, physically,

mentally and spiritually, and the best
will come to you.   5203-1

Do not condemn self. Condemning of
self is as much of an error as
condemning others.   3292-1

In Him there are no limitations. One
only limits self by doubt or fear.   2574-1

Knowledge is not *always* understanding; for these are as knowledge in the
daily experiences that are as miracles,
yet they become so often as everyday
facts that there is no understanding in
the mercies or the glories that are
showered upon the sons of man from an
All-Wise Creator. Few get understanding that have mere knowledge.   262-19

For the beginning of knowledge is to
know self and self's relationship to
God! Then the relationship to the fellow
man; then material knowledge to any

entity, any soul, may *become* valuable,
worthwhile, aggressive, advancing—
success!   1249-1

Let no day then pass that ye do not
speak a *cheery* and an encouraging
word to someone! And ye will find thine
own heart uplifted, thine own life
opened, thy love appreciated, thy
purposes understood!   1754-1

Know, self is the only excuse. Self is
the only sin; that is, selfishness—and
all the others are just a modification of
that expression of the ego. But so close
is the ego, the I Am, to the *Great I Am,
That I Am,* that the confusions of duty
and privilege and opportunity become
so enmeshed in the experience of the
entity.

And so great are the abilities of the
entity to make of this experience a
glory for the living God, that to fail
would be indeed calamitous in the
experience of this soul.   1362-1

. . .those that find fault with others will find fault in themselves; for they are writing their own record—they must meet, every one, that which they have said about another; for so is the image, the soul of the Creator in each body, and when ye speak evil of or unkindly to thy brother, thou hast done it unto thy God.   487-17

Remember the beautiful ever, and look for the agreements rather than for disagreements. Do not condemn that which has not been applied nor that self has not experienced in the same character of circumstance. Thus, never repeat that which might be harmful to anyone, even though it be only gossip for the moment.   1533-2

"Except ye become as little children, ye shall in no wise enter in." Unless you can be just as forgiving, unless you can find it just as easy to forget slights and slurs and things that would make afraid those who would judge others. For with what measure ye mete, it is measured to thee again. Even as He, the Master gave, the faults ye find in others are reflected in thine own mirror of life. And as He gave, "Cast the beam out of thine eye that ye may see to take the mote from thy brother's eye."   3395-2

For, each soul must come to know its *own* influence and that which is the most helpful. And if it calls then for self to cleanse the body without and within with pure water, or to fast, or to burn incense, or to set about self certain odors or colors of influences, then—as has been given—use these for thine *own* development, but be a seeker and a user of that which thou obtainest. For, not only the hearer but rather the doer gains, in its seeking through to the Infinite forces and influences.

Hence, whether it is desired from the experience to abstain from this, that or the other influence to obtain the better conditions in self, seek to know these— for *thou* art not dumb, my brother!
                                            440-12

. . .in love all life is given, in love all things move. In giving one attains. In giving one acquires. In giving love comes as the fulfillment of desire, guided, directed, in the ways that bring the more perfect knowledge of application of self as related to the universal, all powerful, all guiding, all divine influence in life—or it *is* life.   345-1

If one would have friends, one must show self friendly! This is not merely as an idiom, or as a saying, but truth! This should not be merely preached at the entity, but practiced *with* the entity!

                                                    2443-1

For, as thon, the evolution of man's experiences is for the individual purpose of becoming more and more acquainted with those activities in the relationships with the fellow man, as an exemplification, as a manifestation of Divine Love—as was shown by the Son of man, Jesus; that *each* and every soul *must become, must be* the *savior* of some soul! to even *comprehend* the purpose of the entrance of the Son *into* the earth—that man might have the closer walk with, yea the open door to, the very heart of the living God! 1472-3

Try to see self in the other's place. And this will bring the basic spiritual forces that must be the prompting influence in the experience of each soul, if it would grow in grace, in knowledge, in understanding; not only of its relationship to God, its relationship to its fellow man, but its relationships in the home and in the social life. 2936-2

Do not try to assist self, but rather smile upon those that are downhearted and sad; lift the load from those that find theirs too heavy to bear, in gentleness, in kindness, in long-suffering, in patience, in mercy, in brotherly love. And as ye show forth these to thy fellow man, the ways and the gates of glory open before thee. 272-8

From what may *anyone* be saved? Only from themselves! That is, their individual hell; they dig it with their own desires! 262-40

This may be a hard statement for many, but you will eventually come to know it is true: No fault, no hurt comes to self save that thou hast created in thine consciousness, in thine inner self, the cause. For only those that ye love may hurt you. 262-83

Hold rather to those things in which, in thy dealings with thy fellow man, ye may see only the pure, the *good!* For until ye are able to see within the life and activities of those ye have come to hate the most, *something* ye would worship in thy Creator, ye haven't begun to think straight. 1776-1

Take counsel in self. Give unto self that worthy, acceptable period of service, for in service to others, is lending to that Creative Energy that makes or destroys lives. Lives are as worlds, for each is of that material of which the universe is and was created—

for in the life of the entity enters many of those conditions that may be made into miracles or crimes.   2497-3

Rather, then, than the stars *ruling* the life, the life should rule the stars. For man was created a little bit higher than all the rest of the whole universe, and is capable of harnessing, directing, enforcing the laws of the universe   5-2

And when those relationships about same have been and are such that those conditions arise wherein there is the lack of harmonious effects that are possible, then as He hath given, put at naught those experiences, those influences. Let them be rather as they were not.   845-4

For whether ye preach a sermon, or whether ye entertain in those manners as befitting to the activities of the group, let it be done with an eye-singleness of *service*, of *joy*, of helpfulness to thy fellow man.   887-3

Be not overcome with those things that make for discouragements, for *He* will supply the strength. Lean upon the arm of the Divine within thee, giving not place to thoughts of vengeance or discouragements. Give not vent to those things that create prejudice. And, most of all, be *unselfish!* For selfishness is sin, before first thine self, then thine neighbor and thy God.   254-87

Then, keep that. For, none may tell another *how* to be beautiful. It must be the reflection of that entertained in the heart and mind of the individual. And as He is beauty, He is friendship, He is love, the more and the nearer individuals reflect that in their conversation, in their dealings with their fellow man, the greater the glory to Him.   2574-1

The *joy,* the peace, the happiness, that may be ours is in *doing* for the *other* fellow. For, gaining an understanding of the laws as pertain to right living in all its phases makes the mind in attune with *Creative* Forces, which *are* of *His* consciousness. So we may have *that* consciousness, by putting into action *that* we know.   262-3

For, as He taught, and as ye learn more, "Suffer little children to come unto me" is indeed the greater promise to the earth. For unless we become as children we cannot enter in; unless we learn as they. No faults, no hates remain in their experience, until they are taught to manifest such. Hence these may give thee greater insight into the meaning of it all.   1992-1

. . .justifying of self is blaming someone else.   2803-2

For, the error that man makes is the more oft against himself than making for the breaking of law as related to divine influence in the experience. For, love is law—law is love, in its essence. And with the breaking of the law is the making of the necessity for atonement and forgiveness, in that which may take away error to or what has been brought in the experience of the individual.

                    262-45

The Source,
the Pattern,
and the Power

God seeks all to be one with Him. And as all things were made by Him, that which is the creative influence in every herb, every mineral, every vegetable, every individual activity, *is* that same force ye call God—and *seeks* expression! Even as when God said: "Let there be light," and there was light. For, this is law; this is love.   294-202

But know each soul must find its way back to its God. Be as the leader gave of old, "Others may do as they may, but as for me—*I* will serve the *living* God." Not the God of any people, of any individual, but the *living* God—that is personal to those that seek to know Him as a personal God. . .So may the entity, with the spirit of God through the power of the Christ Consciousness, come to know—in *every* thing, in every act— that love that may pass all understandings. For, to others it may be as a myth, as a dream, as a thing to be hoped for, but to this body, to this entity, to this soul, who has tasted of the joys of the personal contact with those influences within the soul, it may come to be His power working within.   255-12

For the entity, as each soul, is a portion of the whole. Thus, though a soul may be as but a speck upon the earth's environs, and the earth in turn much less than a mote in the universe, if the spirit of man is so attuned to the Infinite, the music of harmony becomes as the divine love that makes for the awareness in the experience of the Creative Forces working with self for the knowledge of the associations with same.   1469-1

. . .ye are part and parcel of a Universal Consciousness, or God—and thus of all that is within the universal consciousness or the universal aware-ness, as the stars, the planets, the sun, the moon. Do ye rule them or they rule thee? They were made for thine own use, as an individual—yea, that is the thought which thy Maker, thy Father-God thinks of thee.

For ye are as a corpuscle in the body of God; thus a co-creator with Him in what ye think, in what ye do. And ye change each soul ye contact, literally or mentally—insofar as ye, an individual entity, are a witness for or against the Lord, thy God. . .no soul may come in contact with the entity without being changed either in body, in mind, or in purpose. And purpose is, of course, of the soul!   2794-3

For as the heaven is His throne, the earth is His footstool, so may we at His feet learn, know, become aware of, the knowledge of His ways. For He is not past finding out. For is God, the Father, so far away that He answers our pleas, our prayers, as from afar? Rather is His presence felt when we become aware of His force, His power, His love; the knowledge of His presence in our lives,

our experiences, our undertakings, in
His name.   262-95

Thus the purpose of each experience
is that the entity may magnify and
glorify that which is good. For, good is
of the one source, God, and is eternal.
Then as an individual entity magnifies
that which is good, and minimizes that
which is false, it grows in grace, in
knowledge, in understanding.   2599-1

Watch, that ye be not overcome.
Watch and pray, for as the Father giveth
so does the understanding come as to
what may be accomplished in the
efforts of the self in relationships to
others; and ye are the light-bearers for
Him.   262-26

Thus He that came into the earth as an
example, as a way, is an ideal—is *the*
ideal. They that climb up some other
way become robbers of that peace, that
harmony, which may be theirs—by

being at-one with that He manifested in the earth.   2537-1

That He gave of old is as new today as it was in the beginning of man's relationship or seeking to know the will of God, if ye will but call on Him *within* thine inner *self!* Know that thy body is the temple of the living God. *There* He has promised to meet thee!   281-41

There has been and is ever the promise to every soul that He, thy Father, thy God, will meet thee in thy holy temple. Then accept same. Prepare self. Dedicate self; making those necessary activities for insuring self of that influence, that activity on the part of self, and there needs be little fear— *ever*—to enter. For he that does so doubting already *invites* that which would bring corruption, dissension. But he that does so in the assurance that the promises are true, the promises are

thine *own,* in insuring self and mak...g
secure. 877-2

Whether in joy, in sorrow, in trouble
or in pain, let that mind be in you as was
in He that gave, *"I am with you always,
even unto the end of the world."* 262-33

To *live* love is to be love. To be one
with the Father is to be equal *with* the
Father, and as the understanding of the
entity is gained in the application of
truths gained in the consciousness *of*
truth is apparent—for, as has been
given, to love is to *live* love—not the
answer of desire or of amorous
affection, but is all in one—for love is
law, law is love. 900-331

Hence, in the fruits of that—as is
given oft, as the fruits of the spirit—
does man become aware of the infinite
penetrating, or interpenetrating the
activities of all forces of matter, or that

which is a manifestation of the realm of the infinite into the finite—and the finite becomes conscious of same. 262-52

. . .as God's purpose is to glorify the individual man (or soul) in the earth, so the highest purpose of an individual soul or entity is to glorify the Creative Energy or God in the earth.   338-3

Then we say, when our loved ones, our heart's desires are taken from us, in what are we to believe?

This we find is only answered in that which has been given as His premise, that God hath not willed that any soul should perish but hath with every temptation, every trial, every disappointment made a way of escape or for correcting same. It is not a way of justification only, as by faith, but a way to know, to realize that in these disappointments, separations, there comes the assurance that He cares!

1567-2

Love the Lord. Keep His ways. For He, as ye must always remember, hath blessed thee personally. And that means for keeps!　　　3003-1

Jesus is the man—the activity, the mind, the relationships that He bore to others. Yea, He was mindful of friends, He was sociable, He was loving, He was kind, He was gentle. He grew faint, He grew weak—and yet gained that strength that He has promised, in becoming the Christ, by fulfilling and overcoming the world! Ye are made strong—in body, in mind, in soul and purpose—by that power in Christ. The *power*, then, is in the Christ. The *pattern* is in Jesus.　　　2533-7

They that have ministered that the God-force, the soul that is the image of the Maker *might* be glorified have done so unto the Lord. His brethren, His individual selves are but the material manifestations of that Creative Force in a material world.   524-2

Let the light of His countenance rest upon thee and bring thee peace. Let His ways be thy ways. Let joy and happiness be ever in thy word, in thy song. Let *hopefulness,* helpfulness, ever be thy guide. The Lord is thy shepherd; let Him keep thy ways. 938-1

Each soul's entrance into material consciousness should represent to the entity the awareness that a universal consciousness, God, is aware of the entity's purpose, the entity's aims. And this consciousness represents an opportunity for the entity, in the material experience, to become a channel to glorify that purpose, that cause.   2622-1

For only as ye forgive those who have blamed thee without a cause, who have spoken vilely of thee without reason,

can the giver of life and light forgive
thee—even though He came into
experience that ye, even ye, might know
thy place with God, with thy Maker.

3660-1

And let patience and love be thy
guide. For divine love is that which
makes aware to the hearts and souls of
men the *presence* of His love, of the
Father being within!

528-14

And as He hath given, "If ye love me,
keep my commandments; for they are
not grievous to bear. For I will bear
them with thee, I will wipe away thy
tears; I will comfort the brokenhearted,
I will bring all to those in the ways that
are in the Wisdom of God for thy
expressions through each experience,
in each activity of thine."

For thy soul in its Wisdom seeketh
expression with Him. Smother it not in
the doubts and the fears of materiality
but in the spirit of love and truth that
encompasseth all, and that is open to ye

who have set thy hearts, thy faces,
toward the love that is in Jesus, thy
friend, thy Brother.   262-105

He came, the Master, in flesh and
blood, even as thou didst come in flesh
and blood. Yet as He then proclaimed to
thee, there is a cleansing of the body, of
the flesh, of the blood, in such measures
that it may become illumined with
power from on high; that is *within* thine
own body to WILL! "Thy will, O God; not
mine, but Thine, be done in me and
through me."   1152-1

For all prayer is answered. Don't tell
God how to answer it.   4028-1

He, thy King, thy Lord; yea, thy
Brother hath *shown* thee the way: "*I* am
the way; I am the water of life." Drink ye
deep of same, that the healing you each
may administer to others may flow as
His love through thee! For love healeth
the wounded; it binds up the broken-

hearted; it makes for understandings where differences have arisen. For *God* is love.
688-4

In giving to these, then, that seek to know more of that circumstance, those conditions as surrounded that ye call the first Christmas: Do not confuse thyselves. While to you it may be a first Christmas, if it were the first then there would be a last; and ye would not worship, ye would not hold to that which passeth.

For time never was when there was not a Christ and not a Christ mass.
262-103

Know ye this, each of you: The law of the Lord is perfect, ye cannot get around it. Ye may for the moment submerge it, but thy conscience will smite thee.
2811-3

Who may separate you from the love of the Father? Only thyself. For, an injury that may be done thee—or done thy body—is as being done unto the

Maker, and the *Lord* is the avenger of
those that love Him.   262-65

Cultivate the ability to see the
ridiculous, and to retain the ability to
laugh. For, know—only in those that
God hath favored is there the ability to
laugh, even when clouds of doubt arise,
or when every form of disturbance
arises. For, remember, the Master
smiled—and laughed, oft—even on the
way to Gethsemane.   2984-1

That thou art conscious of being
aware of life, of its troubles, of its joys,
of its sorrows, of its peace, of its
fulfillment, should indicate and make
aware in thine own consciousness the
glory of God, that He is mindful of thee.
And, as ye mete to thy brethren day by
day, so do ye unto thy Lord and thy God.
For, as ye measure unto others, it is
measured to thee again.   3213-1

[Karmic conditions] can be met most
in Him who, taking away the law of
cause and effect by fulfilling the law,

establishes the law of grace. Thus the
needs for the entity to lean upon the arm
of Him who is the law, and the truth and
the light.   2828-4

Ye, too, oft doubt; ye, too, oft fear. Yet
He is surely with thee. And when ye at
this glad season rededicate thy life, thy
body, thy mind to His service, ye—too—
may know, as they, that He *lives*—and
is at the right hand of God to make
intercession for *you*—if ye will believe;
if ye will believe that He is, ye may
experience. For as many as have named
the name, and that do unto their
brethren the deeds that bring to them (to
you) that closeness, oneness of purpose
with Him, may know—ye, too—in body,
in mind, that He *lives today,* and will
come and receive you unto Himself,
that where He is there ye may be also.
                                              5749-6

. . .for being afraid is the first
consciousness of sin's entering in, for
he that is made afraid has lost
consciousness of self's own heritage
with the Son; for we are heirs through

Him to that Kingdom that is beyond all
of that that would make afraid or that
would cause a doubt in the heart of any.
243-10

Infinite Love is the Love of God, while
Love Divine is that manifested by those
in their activities who are guided by
love divine. These bring happiness and
the experiences of joy; not mere
pleasure, not gratification of any of the
material things. But differentiate—or,
as has been given—put the proper value
upon the proper phases of one's
experience.   262-11

Keep that awareness of His presence.
For, as He hath given, "Lo, I am with
you always, even unto the end of the
world." And though there may be
abroad hate, avarice, selfishness, and
those things that make man afraid—be
still within thine own heart, thine own
consciousness, and know that He is
with thee.   281-59

There is the necessity that the physical body be in as perfect accord with the Creative and Universal Forces as is possible, but "Thy will be done in me as Thou seest I have need of in the present. Let me bear in my body those conditions, circumstances, physical *and* mental, that will bring me wholly closer to an understanding of the purposes for which I came into being; without censure to anyone, without censure to myself, but *use* me as *Thou* seest fit!" 5640-3

"I will not leave thee comfortless, but will come and *enjoin* thee in thy daily activities, thy daily service." This is the promise to every soul. If ye would make that promise thine own, then seek and ye shall find, knock and it shall be opened unto thee. Let there be definite periods [in] which ye look within self, cleansing the mind, the body, in such ways and manners and measures that

seemeth that as ye would offer as thine
offering unto the holy experiences that
may be thine. For, he that expects
nothing shall not be disappointed, but
he that expects much—if he lives and
uses that in hand day by day—shall be
full to running over. For the love of the
Father constraineth thee to keep thine
counsel with those thou meetest day by
day that thou mayest aid. Thus may the
soul find expression. Thus may the life,
the experience, that portion of life thou
has in this present experience become
more and more beautiful, and the
sunshine of thy love into the hearts and
souls of those that are wondering, that
are troubled because they find not the
spirit of truth and life in *their* own lives,
wilt come into those experiences of
calling thee *blessed* in the name of the
Father.   557-3

Then let it be a personal thing to thee,
that He is thy strength, He *is* thy life!
For in Him ye live and move and have
thy being!   528-13

For a man is a little lower than the angels, yet was made that he might become the companion of the Creative Forces; and thus was given—in the breath of life—the individual soul, the stamp of approval, as it were, of the Creator; with the ability to know itself, and to make itself as one with the Creative Forces—IRRESPECTIVE of other influences. 1456-1

Q-1. What is God's plan for me in assisting the furtherance of His kingdom here on this planet, so that I may accomplish the greatest good with whatever talents I may possess?

A-1. Brighten the corner where thou art from day to day. Let not a day go by without speaking to someone with the smile of the face and eye reminding them that somebody cares, and it is Jesus! 3357-1

THE WORK OF EDGAR CAYCE TODAY

The Association for Research and Enlightenment, Inc. (A.R.E.®), is a membership organization founded by Edgar Cayce in 1931.

• 14,256 Cayce readings, the largest body of documented psychic information anywhere in the world, are housed in the A.R.E. Library/Conference Center in Virginia Beach, Virginia. These readings have been indexed under 10,000 different topics and are open to the public.

• An attractive package of membership benefits is available for modest yearly dues. Benefits include: a bi-monthly magazine; lessons for home study; a lending library through the mail, which offers collections of the actual readings as well as one of the world's best parapsychological book collections, names of doctors or health care professionals in your area.

• As an organization on the leading edge in exciting new fields, A.R.E. presents a selection of publications and seminars by prominent authorities in the fields covered, exploring such areas as parapsychology, dreams, meditation, world religions, holistic health, reincarnation and life after death, and personal growth.

• The unique path to personal growth outlined in the Cayce readings is developed through a worldwide program of study groups. These informal groups meet weekly in private homes.

• A.R.E. maintains a visitors' center where a bookstore, exhibits, classes, a movie, and audiovisual presentations introduce inquirers to concepts from the Cayce readings.

• A.R.E. conducts research into the helpfulness of both the medical and nonmedical readings, often giving members the opportunity to participate in the studies.

For more information and a color brochure, write or phone:

A.R.E., P.O. Box 595, 67th Street and Atlantic Avenue,
Virginia Beach, VA 23451, (804) 428-3588